ENJOYING GARDEN MOMENTS
with THOSE YOU LOVE

A Flower for My Friend

Alda Ellis

HARVEST HOUSE PUBLISHERS
EUGENE, OREGON

A Flower for My Friend
Copyright © 2002 by Alda Ellis
Published by Harvest House Publishers
Eugene, OR 97402

Library of Congress Cataloging-in-Publication Data
Ellis, Alda, 1952-
   A flower for my friend/Alda Ellis.
      p. cm.
   ISBN 0-7369-0573-1
    1. Gardening. I. Title.
SB455 .E56 2002
635.9-dc21

2001038507

Artwork which appears in this book is from the personal collection of Alda Ellis.

Design and Production by Left Coast Design, Portland, Oregon

Unless otherwise indicated, verses are taken from the Revised Standard Version of the Bible, Copyright © 1946, 1952, 1971 by the Division of Christian Education of the National Council of the Churches of Christ in the U.S.A. Used by permission.

Verses marked KJV are from the King James Version of the Bible.

Printed in China

02 03 04 05 06 07 08 09 10 11 12/ IM /10 9 8 7 6 5 4 3 2 1

Dedicated to

my lifelong gardening friend, Renee Hurd
my love of gardening friend, Debra Rightmire
my horticulture friend, Demi Penor
my gardening sister, Cheryl Johnson
and my patient husband, for mowing around my flowers

Contents

1. The Promise of a Garden 7

2. Familiar as an Old Friend 15

3. Scenes of Serenity 31

4. A Garden for All Seasons 45

5. Wonders Never Cease 57

6. A Bouquet of Gatherings 67

Oh, Adam was a gardener,
and God who made him sees
That half a proper gardener's
work is done upon his knees,
So when your work is finished,
You can wash your hands and pray
For the Glory of the Garden,
that it may not pass away!

RUDYARD KIPLING

1
The Promise of a Garden

My grandfather was a farmer and my parents were avid gardeners, so quite naturally I like to dig in the dirt. As a small child it was revealed to me that with every seed planted, there comes the hope of something wonderful—the promise of a garden.

Gardening is rewarding in the most basic of ways, for not only do we get to see the results of our efforts, we also get to feel them. The act of gardening connects our souls to the earth. It connects us to friends with whom we share our abundance of seeds, divisions, and bounty. It connects us to our families as we enjoy a feast of flowers for the eyes or a bounty of vegetables for the table. A garden keeps us grounded, helping us to release daily stress. And just like

> *Be rooted and grounded in love.*
> **THE BOOK OF EPHESIANS**

all gardeners,
all gardens are
unique. The
common thread
that ties us all
together are the
blessings of hope,
faith, discovery,
and joy that we
find in the garden.
When we moved
into our home twenty-one
years ago, it never occurred to
me that I
would enjoy
it more today
than on the day
we moved in.

*All my hurts my
garden can heal.*

RALPH WALDO
EMERSON

The years of hard
work put into
projects and the
memories of celebra-
tions and gatherings are, of course, part of what
make a house a home. Still, ours is a work in progress,
for we always seem to have inspiration to improve something,
change another thing, or simply to plant something new.

We have done our best to maintain the dignity of this historic home, and it is the surroundings that are most dear to my heart. Bendy willow trees, rose of Sharon, mighty oaks, and grand magnolia trees—all original, turn-of-the-century plantings—are still lovingly cherished and maintained today. The grandfather oak tree, with its limbs reaching far and wide, has watched children grow up beneath its branches. It has been ravaged by a tornado yet still stands firm, and it has silently watched the traffic on the road in front of our home change from horses and buggies to cars and FedEx trucks. Like this tree, certain elements of a garden are constant, a hundred years ago or today—a puddle of sunlight, the chirp of a bird's song, a family of nesting squirrels, a burst of color as the seasons change.

A MEMORY TREE

Plant a tree in celebration of the birth of a child. Looking out my kitchen window every morning, I see two very special trees. Each tree was planted in celebration the year my sons were born. I chose cedar for both Mason and Samuel because cedar—an evergreen—stays green all year long. Each year at the start of school, I take a picture of each boy standing in front of his very own tree. At Christmas the boys decorate their trees for the birds with peanut butter and birdseed. For a few short years, the boys were actually taller than their special tree, but the trees now tower above their heads. With Mason heading off to college this fall, I am ever so thankful for his tree of memories.

The quiet memories of the past echo in the ivy-clad stone wall that greets all who enter our timeworn iron gates. The jonquil bulbs have multiplied their numbers to hundreds, and a massive dogwood tree bursts forth each spring in glorious bloom, whispering past secrets of

garden joys. The hundred-year-old red oak tree still sends forth its wide-stretching limbs to hold a sturdy rope swing that sweeps out over the lake. The swing used to get taken for daily rides, but now it spends most days motionless, for my sons have grown too big and too busy to rise high in the wind.

Walking through our pasture to the barn, I pass an elm tree that is encircled by a bed of sleeping iris bulbs. The flowers will bloom for me for the first time this year. I can't wait to see their colors, for each one reminds me of a special time and a special friend. It was almost a year ago that my friend Debra and I lovingly dug up each prized iris bulb from her yard. Debra was in the process of moving from the house where she had raised her two daughters. She was moving to my city and in with our family until she could get settled in a new home. Debra settled into our guest house, and during that time I dearly loved having a "neighbor," for we live in the country and our closest neighbor lives far down the road. Along with some furnishings, Debra brought with her photos of her girls, assorted antique flowerpots, iris, hostas, Christmas cactus, and ferns.

The pain of leaving a place you love is made easier by bringing a piece of it with you. The iris—which some call *fleur-de-lis*—that encircle my elm tree may be the emblem of the French monarchy, but to me they are the emblem of friendship. Debra and I have laughed together, cried together, and now we work together as she and her daughters live nearby in a new home. Today, the hostas are leafing and the fern fronds are unfolding just as the iris are ready to begin blooming. The promises of friendship unfold beautifully in a garden of joy.

Perhaps it is the blue spruce planted in our front yard, once the living room Christmas tree and now twice as tall as our two-story house.

PLANT A TREE FOR THE ENVIRONMENT

Trees not only help to remind us of someone dear, they also help to clean the air by removing carbon dioxide from the atmosphere. They give us shade from the sultry summer sun. They are esthetically pleasing to any newly-built dwelling, for they instantly give a home character. The roots of the trees help to stabilize the ground, especially important in flood-prone areas. For birds, squirrels, and all sorts of small wildlife, trees provide both food and shelter.

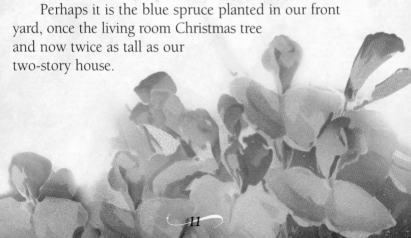

PLANT A TREE
FOR THE FUTURE

A tree planted for future generations is a way for anyone to leave something for posterity. When visiting Gettysburg, Mason and I stood in awe underneath the same honey locust tree where Abraham Lincoln delivered the Gettysburg address. A live oak planted at the Alamo after the deaths of Sam Houston and Davy Crockett lets us actually reach out and touch the past. Planting a tree is not only a great family activity, but it is a most memorable way to mark an event, anniversary, birth, or loss.

It has been said that when people plant a tree, they plant a part of themselves. I called my father, who just turned eighty-nine, this morning and asked him what he would be doing today. He said that he would be busy cleaning up his yard from the hard windstorm we had earlier in the week. He spoke of how sad and distraught he was that the past winter's ice storm had ravaged, broken, and destroyed so many of his trees. But for today, he tells me that he is going to work in his garden and plant a row of corn. Then he stunned me with his next question: "What kind of tree do you think I need to plant in the yard?" Now, what miraculous, wonderful faith that at his age, he wants to plant a tree!

Maybe it is the two cedar trees planted on the month and year each of my sons was born. Possibly it is the rosebush that made the journey from my great-grandmother's home place, or Debra's iris that encircle the elm tree. Maybe it is the moss gathered from a long-ago canoe trip on the War Eagle River. I consider all of these treasures, and realize that garden promises are fulfilled in the flowering of family and friendship.

12

PLANT A TREE TO REMEMBER SOMEONE SPECIAL

I planted a plum tree the year I lost my mother. Beautiful in its crimson foliage, it now bears fruit. Mother would have loved the delicate pink blossoms that burst forth each spring. During this difficult time, our family dentist sent us a gift certificate from a local nursery for a pink dogwood tree. That, too, is a lovely living reminder of my mother's life.

Kind hearts are the gardens.
Kind thoughts are the roots.
Kind words are the flowers.
Kind deeds are the fruit.
Take care of the gardens,
and keep them from weeds.
Fill, fill them with flowers,
kind words, and kind deeds.

HENRY WADSWORTH
LONGFELLOW

2
Familiar as an Old Friend

My favorite gardening tools are my grandfather's shovel and my mother's hand spade. The wood on the handles has been lovingly worn smooth from years of use, and the metal shines from the mountains of dirt they must have moved, for both were such avid gardeners. Vegetable gardens and flower gardens were the fruits of their labor, and even though these favored tools may be well-worn with age, they are still quite comfortable to use. I think that's because they have aged with such fond memories— walking the rows with my grandfather, being held in the gentle hands of my mother.

15

The Serenity of a Watering Can

Old watering cans are such links to the
past. If I happen upon one when I'm out on
an antique jaunt, I usually bring it home,
for they are not only useful watering tools
but are also charming containers for
holding bountiful bouquets of flowers.
I like to place large ones at the front
door near the outdoor dining area and
use smaller ones for table centerpieces.
Fistfuls of wildflowers, weeds, and
grasses make for a quick and easy
flower arrangement no matter what
the season. Even in the fall, I fill them
with brightly colored leaves, rose hips,
twirly vines, and interesting berries.

Out in the Gardening Shed

Over the years I have enjoyed collecting old tools
from antique shops and tag sales. Their lovely wooden
handles are so much more appealing than the plastic ones
of today. Some are too rusted to use properly, so I put
them to work decorating a wall of my tool shed. Artistically
collected and arranged, they add charm and a touch of the
past to even the simplest of gardening sheds. Sometimes
they can be purchased for very little money, and with a bit
of oil on the handle and steel wool on the metal, they are
truly charming. As familiar as an old friend, at one time
they perhaps planted heirloom tomatoes or raked autumn's
kaleidoscope of leaves.

No Friend Like an Old Friend

It takes years of watering for a terra-cotta pot to accumulate the lovely patina of moss and mineral deposits which give it that well-worn look. In a grouping of old pots, a new clay pot sticks out like a sore thumb. Yard sales and tag sales used to be full of old ones, but now it seems that everyone is scooping them up. They look so pretty, even casually displayed upside-down on a gardening bench. When I can't find old pots with well-worn finishes, I like to "age" my new clay pots. If I have

TIMEWORN TERRA-COTTA POTS

To create a timeworn pot, immerse the pot in water and let it become quite absorbed. In the natural aging process, there are at least three varieties of colors that accumulate on a pot—white, a deep shade of moss green, and brown.

First, very lightly dab white latex paint with a wet rag on the pot in a random way to imitate mineral deposits. For the second color of deep moss green, dip a different rag in the latex paint and "pat" on the moss. Pat especially around the bottom one-fourth of the pot where much of the moss would naturally collect. Also pat the green paint under the top rim, in the crease of the pot, for that too is where the pot would naturally collect moisture.

For the third color, dip another rag into the water and squeeze out the moisture. Ever so lightly, dip it into a shade of brown. Pat the brown on gently so the colors will not turn to "mud" but will instead create the richness of an aged patina.

Allow to dry—and enjoy!

time, I paint them with buttermilk and yogurt and then "age" them in a plastic bag. But sometimes I am in a hurry and need an aged pot right away, so then I treat them with a painting technique. And as long as I have my hands in the paint, I often treat a few extra pots to give as gift "baskets" to my gardening friends.

Friendship's Garden

Some of my favorite flowers have not come from seed catalogs or nurseries, but from friends who delight in sharing their love of gardening with me. Snippets of creeping Jenny that line my water garden, root cuttings of hydrangeas, seeds mailed in an envelope across the miles—all are much more valuable to me than any nursery's offerings.

So deeply is the gardener's instinct implanted in my soul, I really love the tools with which I work—the iron fork, the spade, the hoe, the rake, the trowel, and the watering-pot are pleasant objects in my eyes.

CELIA THAXTER

Every time I brush by the peony bush near my back door, I think of my friend Mary. I so treasure this pink peony, for it represents how Mary gave both time and energy as she worked to divide the plant with me. She is always giving me roots, plants, and cuttings, and as these new plants have been added to my garden, I have seen unfold a beautiful picture of the flowering of our friendship. Growing enough of a particular plant to share with a friend is both a gardening pleasure and a gift of friendship.

I love to visit the gardens of friends. One Sunday afternoon I was treated to lunch in my friend Beth's new town home. She told me that after we ate, she would give me a garden tour. I was delighted to find in such a tiny space an abundance of inspiration. She and her next-door neighbor had managed to bring in rock and soil and create a cutting garden in the tiny, tiny space between their homes. We visited with Beth's neighbor, who was working alongside a wheelbarrow in her wide-brimmed straw hat as she kneeled to tidy the garden.

The tiny space has become a venue for sharing with other neighbors, and neighborly swapping of plants is organized for the fall. Because Beth travels so much, she thinks it is especially nice to have her neighbor's help in looking after and watering the garden when she is away for a week or more.

TOOLS OF MY FRIENDSHIP GARDEN

The Wheelbarrow…to bear a load when it is too much for us to carry alone.

The Trowel…to break up the soil, encouraging the roots of friendship to grow deeper. It separates the weeds so they can be tossed and friendship's flower nurtured.

A Rake…to make tidy and neat our friendship gardens and help gather up what needs to be carried away.

A Watering Can…to replenish and nurture as it spills out on friendship's plantings.

Beth and her neighbor have also become closer friends as they share the pleasures of gardening as well as the gerbera and Shasta daisies that brighten their kitchen tables and warm their hearts.

Our gardens can also keep long-distance friendships strong. One very special Christmas card I look forward to receiving every year is from my friend Patty. It holds not only a cheery holiday greeting but also a packet of seeds, which varies from year to year. This year's were bright red coleus. They are a symbol of our gardening friendship, a gift

to be planted as the year goes forth. Patty's seeds serve as a reminder of Christmas kindness, even in the middle of summer.

Plants that need to be divided such as daylilies, iris, and cannas surely are meant to be shared with gardening friends. My cannas came from my friend Renee's garden, probably because I had shared some wisteria vine with her one Sunday afternoon.

*Thoughts of thee are
with me ever,
Near to thee and far apart,
Like fair blossoms
fading never,
In the garden of my heart.*

AUTHOR UNKNOWN

Along the edge of our woods, the wisteria vines grow rampant and plentiful. One year the wisteria was so abundant that Renee decided to take another armload of vines to our friend Carol. But to my disbelief, Renee came back up the hill with poison ivy vines instead of the intended wisteria! After a quick washing of hands and arms in a mild bleach solution, Renee decided that she'd collected enough. We still laugh when we remember the armload of poison ivy vines she was going to plant. Now an elementary school teacher, Renee has been my friend since childhood. She is always nearby when I need her, and our endearing friendship has blossomed through the years as too have our gardens.

Peonies from Mary, iris from Debra, cannas from Renee—these are the treasures of my friendship garden.

Family Gardens

The vintage blush pink rose that will reach the top of my trellis this year was salvaged and given to me by a favorite uncle. Well over a hundred years old, this ancestral cutting came from my great-grandmother's home place where she had raised four sons. By her front steps grew the pretty-as-a-painting rosebush that she so lovingly tended.

With its heady fragrance and full foliage and buds, this disease-resistant and drought-tolerant plant puts to shame some of my designer hybrid tea roses.

*More than anything,
I must have flowers,
always, always.*

CLAUDE MONET

My rose garden is home to several different varieties of roses. Each spring, I look forward to their budding, as I enjoy tending them and planting new ones. In the corner of the rose garden is a bush that once lay dormant after leaves and buds were full on the others. I decided to give it a bit more time before pulling it up, and finally I began to see tiny green leaves on the plant. The process reminded me that sometimes, as a friend and as a parent, I may give up too soon. Everything—plants, children, friendships—blooms at its own pace, and I must remember to allow each sufficient time if I am to gather a bouquet of roses.

The antique rosebush on my father's fence is buried in bloom. Over the years I have watched it graciously fill with blossoms as one of the rites of spring. Shrub roses fit so comfortably on a fence, and I am delighted that these old-fashioned beauties are now coming back in style. The white varieties are my favorite, for at dusk they set a scene of serenity. As familiar as an old friend, these antique roses are quite different from the long-stemmed varieties that florists now use, for they are so abundant with fragrance. Rose-tangled doorways and cottage trellis displays are easily made possible with antique roses, and they are especially treasured when they have been passed from one generation to the next. If antique roses are not in your own family's history, gardening catalogs and nurseries are helpful places to start your own family tradition of handing down roses.

Children seem to enjoy the gardening hobby at an early age. When Samuel was five or so, he wanted to work right beside me in the garden and plant some seeds. Rather hesitant about turning him loose with the tiny envelope of expensive seeds from the mail order catalog, I said, "Samuel, I'll go get you some great seeds." I ran into the house and reached inside the kitchen cupboard. Then I unscrewed the lid of a jar and poured a handful of seeds into my pocket. I returned to Samuel and, to his delight, placed in his little hand several plump and shiny golden popcorn kernels.

Later in the week, when visiting his grandparents, Samuel asked his grand-mother for some seeds to plant. She replied that she did not think she had any, but he told her he knew where she kept them. Opening her cupboard door, he unscrewed the lid of a jar and shook out a few popcorn kernels.

Like just about all little boys, Samuel loved to dig in the dirt. He had already discovered by digging with Papa's trowel that the softest dirt was around Mom's impatiens, so that is where he decided to plant his popcorn seeds. The perfectly manicured "Lawn of the Month" now had corn planted in the flower bed of boxwood and impatiens!

As summer progressed, the corn quickly grew. Anyone visiting Papa and Mom could not help but notice and ask, "Are those cornstalks growing in your flower bed?" The corn, thriving on the impatiens' fertilizer, grew tall and tasseled. Samuel proudly picked his ear of corn that summer, sharing with us all the joy of his garden.

Living with the luxury of plenty of space, each of my sons has been allowed their own garden spot. I offer suggestions, but I always let them choose what to plant and tend.

Samuel always chooses a variety of flowers—including giant sunflowers—and a few tomato plants. Mason plants two or three kinds of vegetables and lots of strawberry plants—his favorite to eat. Even now, Samuel has seeds sprouting on our windowsill to try to get a jump start on spring—and on his brother's garden. I treasure the time spent working alongside them in their gardens, and they are so delighted when the vegetables, strawberries, and flowers are ripe for the picking.

A Long Vine of Love

One summer when the boys were little, we made a very simple teepee out of bamboo. Leaning the bamboo canes together in a teepee shape, we tied the top shut with honey-suckle vines. We then planted morning glories all around the base of our teepee. They quickly grew and covered the canes, creating a memorable summer hideaway. Beans could also be planted at the base, and the fun would continue as they were picked, cooked, and eaten!

A salad garden is pretty and fun for both children and adults. A galvanized washtub is the perfect size to fill with dirt and plant all sorts of lettuce seed in. Take a trip to the seed store to choose three or four varieties of lettuce. Then pour all the seeds together in a large salt shaker and mix them up, covering the holes with your hand to keep the seeds in. Prepare the dirt in the washtub. If the tub is on a deck or balcony and might eventually need to be moved, it can be made much lighter by adding a layer of

Happiness held is the seed; happiness shared is the flower.

AUTHOR UNKNOWN

empty soda cans and a layer of Styrofoam packing peanuts to the bottom. Top it off with topsoil and sprinkle the salt shaker full of assorted lettuce seeds over the top. Then cover the seeds with dirt and keep your salad garden well watered. The fun is in the picking when your "mixed" green salad starts growing!

Gardens for Everyone

Gardening continues to grow in popularity, and it can be available to almost everyone who has space even for a window box garden, a rooftop garden, or a balcony garden. City dwellers in brownstones can be quite productive gardeners with a seed, a spade, and a little bit of soil. Children of all ages love to have a garden at a windowsill just their height or to see their old wading pool turned into an abundant garden.

A kitchen cupboard can give you what you need to create a special garden for children. They'll be able to watch the miracle of something growing from a seed and also take part in the fun of eating something that they have grown themselves.

One of the easiest crops to grow is a jar full of alfalfa sprouts. I just love them, for they are a delicious way to top off a salad or sandwich. Although beans can be sprouted too, alfalfa sprouts are easy to grow and packed with vitamins. You will need just a few items for your sprout garden—two generous tablespoonfuls of untreated alfalfa seeds, one clean, wide-mouthed-glass jar (such as an old mayonnaise jar), a six-inch square of cheesecloth, and a rubber band.

First, place the alfalfa seeds in the bottom of the jar and fill it halfway with water. Then place the cheesecloth over the mouth of the jar, securing it shut with a rubber band. Store in a dark place, such as the kitchen cupboard shelf. Twice a day, with the cheesecloth lid in place, empty out the water and replace it with fresh water. In about four

LOSING WEIGHT

To lighten the load in any large pot—from high-grade Italian terra-cotta pots to a child's plastic wading pool—fill the bottom third of your container with Styrofoam packing peanuts. Cover the peanuts with a thick layer of newspaper to keep the soil from settling down too far and coming out the drainage holes. The water will flow through the newspaper and it will deteriorate on its own. Fill the rest of the container with potting soil and enjoy losing weight!

The love of gardening is a seed that once sown never dies.

GERTRUDE JEKYLL

days, the sprouts will be ready to eat. Pour off all the water and store your sprouts with a damp paper towel in the refrigerator. Then just add them to your favorite salads and sandwiches!

I have learned so much about gardening over the years from my father. He taught me to wait to plant corn in the spring—"until the oak leaves are as big as squirrel ears." As a child, he taught me early on the names of plants as we walked hand in hand—milkweed, goldenrod, Buckeye bush. About planting perennials, he says, "The first year they sleep, the second year they creep, and the third year they leap!" When buttercups bloom, it is time to plant peas. When the dandelions bloom, it is time to plant beets and carrots. And when the dogwood tree is in full bloom, it is time to plant tomatoes. As the love of gardening is passed from one generation to the next, so too are its lessons.

The old *Farmer's Almanac* is fun to read with its predictions and advice, but the wisdom from my father has given me the memories that flourish in my garden along with my flowers and vegetables.

Fun Theme Gardens for Children

WILD ANIMAL GARDEN

Elephant Ears
Snapdragons
Polar Bear Zinnia
Tiger Baby Watermelon
Bengal Tiger Cannas
Leopard's Bane
Zebra Grass
Foxglove
Kangaroo Vine
Monkey Grass
Rattlesnake Fern

CHOCOLATE GARDEN

Chocolate Mint
Cocoa Grass
Cocoa Palm

BIRDS AND BUGS GARDEN

Cardinal Flower
Butterfly Weed
Bee Balm
Spider Plant
Toadstool
Spiderwort
Turtlehead
Catchfly
Tickseed
Canarybird Flower
Bird's Eye
Devil's Walking Stick
Ragged Robin
Spiderfern
Parrot Tulips

DOG AND CAT GARDEN

Cattails
Pussy Willow
Catnip
Catmint
Dogwood Tree
Dogstooth Violet

FARM ANIMAL GARDEN

Pussy Willow
Cattail
Goatsbeard
Lamb's Ear
Hens and Chicks
Toadlily
Foxtail Lily
Cockscomb
Mare's Tail Grass
Oxeye Daisy
Brown Turkey Fig Tree
Piggyback Plant

You care for the land and water it;
you enrich it abundantly.
The streams of God are
filled with water.

THE BOOK OF PSALMS

3

Scenes of Serenity

O ne of the greatest joys in my garden has been the addition of the element of water. Yes, we did add a swimming pool to entertain teenagers, but that is not what I am referring to. This water was for the garden. A simple birdbath or an elaborate backyard pond adds such serenity to a garden. Not only is the water soothing to see and hear, but it also attracts birds, butterflies, and wildlife to the landscape.

One sultry summer, my husband hired a stonemason to build me a water garden. Our seemingly simple backyard project became a major undertaking. What started out a little fish pond turned into waterfalls, ponds, and a lengthy, meandering hillside stream. The water was to be pumped up our hill from the lake below and spill out into a spring-like pond under an oak tree near the back door. The stonemason created a natural flowing stream that pooled, meandered, and pooled again, along with several little waterfalls cascading down the hill. That was several

years ago, and the stonework was finally finished late that summer. Yet today, the water garden is still my delightful work in progress.

The water garden has added such joy to my gardening. Hostas, ferns, and white impatiens soften the edges of the stonework. The simple element of trickling water over rocks, aquatic hyacinths, lilies, and cannas has resulted in such an oasis of calm. The garden is shaded from the hot summer sun, so it is an easy spot in which to coax almost anything to grow. My plantings have increased abundantly each year, for the hostas, ferns, and decorative grasses thrive on the moisture. Moss dug up from deep in the woods and tucked into cracks and crevices add softness, richness, and detail to the fountain and stepping stone path. Gardens, we are told, are supposed to have "bones." The water element is the

Flowers always make people better, happier and more helpful. They are sunshine, food, and medicine for the soul.

LUTHER BURBANK

backbone of my garden, and my goal is to make it look as if it has always serenely been there. I choose to use only green and white flowers and plants in my water garden. The white flowers are visible even in the moonlight and help to create a peaceful setting. I even call it a Moonlight Garden, for after working all day, it is usually in the evening hours when we enjoy it the most.

Water gardens are actually low maintenance, except for the fact that mine seems to be a creative inspiration on a daily basis. I take such delight in finding a new variety of hosta, fern, or other plant. The endless availability of water garden plants and fish varieties makes for an evolving inspirational setting.

Hurt no living thing;
Ladybird, nor butterfly,
Nor moth with dusty wing,
Nor cricket chirping
cheerily,
Nor grasshopper
so light of leap,
Nor dancing gnat,
nor beetle fat,
Nor harmless worms
that creep.

CHRISTINA ROSSETTI

Our water garden has proved to be a sanctuary for nearby wildlife. Not only do fish and frogs swim in the water, but an assortment of birds is also attracted to the area. Dragonflies, butterflies, frogs, and tadpoles all make their home in my water garden.

With the addition of wildlife comes a symphony of sounds. The sound of the water itself is background music to the night noises of frogs and crickets. The owl that lives across our lake echoes his "hoot-hoot" through the still night air. I always stop what I am doing just to listen to his call.

Since I have added water and stones to my garden, I have noticed how many more butterfly visitors I now receive. It seems a water garden is most attractive to butterflies, for they like to dine on the nearby flowers, drink the water, and warm their wings on the sunny stones.

History tells us that water gardening actually dates back to the Middle Ages when Europeans with large gardens created lily-filled reflecting pools. Today, all you need for a water garden is a container and your imagination. Many stores offer water fountains of some sort, and it is easy to find one that is just right for your garden taste, whether indoors or out. The

For mine is just a little old-fashioned garden where the flowers come together to praise the Lord and teach all who look upon them to do likewise.

CELIA THAXTER

smaller, less expensive pumps make my imagination run, for nearly anything that can hold liquid is a potential water garden. All sorts of containers, wooden barrels, terra-cotta pots, ceramic bowls, and pottery of all shapes and sizes lend themselves to becoming a water garden.

Charming, pre-made water gardens require you to only add water and plug in the pump, but I have found that creating my own water garden has been most rewarding. I love to hear the sound of the water trickling over the lichen-covered rocks and rest my eyes upon the lacy ferns, many varieties of hostas, and impatiens buried in bloom.

A violet by a mossy stone,
Half hidden from the eye,
Fair as a star,
when only one
Is shining from the sky.

WILLIAM
WORDSWORTH

The delightful reflections on the surface of the water add an element of style to any seasonal foliage. Fragrant and colorful exotic plants associated with water gardening add an interesting element of surprise. Even seashells gathered from summers spent at the beach and placed in the water garden by my sons recall scenes of serenity.

I discovered a most memorable container garden inside a courtyard just outside the door of a hotel I stayed at in New Orleans. The water was held in a two-foot diameter terra-cotta vessel covered with velvety moss. Several blades of ornamental grass rising up from the water graced the home of the two tiny goldfish that swam just below the surface. The steamy New Orleans weather was cooled by this tranquil spot of inspiration, and its simplicity made it so charming. Big waterfall, small fountain, or simple container garden—the soothing sound of trickling water calms our senses.

It is not even mandatory to have a pump in your water garden. The beauty of a water feature in the garden is that it can be anything you want it to be. Peaceful, still water in a container nestled into the corner of a flower-filled patio can be just as tranquil as a backyard pond. Floating candles in the still water add to party decor or an evening's idyll. A single camellia bloom, assorted cheerful pansies, or a grand magnolia blossom will last for several days floating in water. A beautiful, peaceful water garden retreat helps soothe our spirit and adds a sense of calm to our lives.

A simple terra-cotta container filled with water brings a sense of tranquility to a garden when its surface reflects its surroundings or simply the pattern of clouds in the sky. By filling a terra-cotta saucer with water, you can have a miniature water garden on a balcony, windowsill, porch, patio, or city garden plot. Birds and butterflies will enjoy a drink from the shallow pool, and some plants will even live in this environment. Duckweed loves still water and grows quickly as it covers the water's surface with its lacy green leaves. Its tiny roots dangle down in the water for fish to nibble on. Even the smallest bit of water adds such a soothing element of serenity.

A Most Welcome Guest

I used to always cringe when I discovered that one of my terra-cotta pots had become cracked and broken. Now I treasure these pots, for I have discovered that they help welcome toads into my garden. Mosquitoes and other unwanted bugs abound in a water garden, so it is a pleasure to provide shelter from a summer thunderstorm for a toad that feasts on such pests.

*When daisies pied
and violets blue
And lady-smocks
all silver white
And cuckoo buds
of yellow hue
Do paint the meadows
with delight.*

WILLIAM
SHAKESPEARE

With water at ground level, the toads are provided with a place to lay their eggs and produce another generation. Samuel and I watch as the tadpoles grow before our eyes in the water garden. Adding to our pleasure in the garden is the joy of discovery, for a broken terra-cotta flowerpot, turned on its side and partially buried in the ground, transforms into a friendly home for garden critters.

Besides toads, I also like to attract beneficial bugs to my garden. A planting of dill, spearmint, basil, and marigolds will attract the right kind of insects. Ladybugs are sure to love these plants! Mother used to sprinkle bran in her flower beds to control the snails. I tried it too, and it seems to really work. I love natural alternatives to pest control.

A Seashell Garden

Treasures from the sea, brought home to remember vacation days long after they have passed, bring joy to your garden. Grouped together, shells make more of a statement than if spread randomly. On some I use a

permanent felt tip pen to record the year and the place—
Sanibel Island, 1996.

Around the edge of a water garden, shells look most appropriate. If the shell is large enough, I am able to fill it with dirt and plant a small fern or moss in it. This makes for an interesting, memorable, and personal flowerpot.

A Butterfly Garden

My husband and I love to horseback ride, and one of our favorite trails is an old, long-abandoned Civil War wagon road that is narrowly nestled between two mountains. A mossy, shady stream runs alongside it. The trail is always full of signs of prior visitors, such as raccoon and fox footprints in the mud. To our surprise one Sunday afternoon, unusual visitors were in full view. Cheyenne and Old Major, our horses, knew the trail quite well, but even they stopped and lifted their heads, noticing something different. Fluttering up ahead was a congregation of monarch butterflies, numbering in the

RECIPE FOR A BUTTERFLY GARDEN

For a beautiful butterfly garden, you simply need a shallow container of water, a few large, flat stones placed in a sunny spot, and some of the following butterfly-attracting flowers—

Bee Balm
Zinnia
Lavender
Phlox
Cosmos
Purple Coneflower
White Daisies
Queen Anne's Lace

hundreds. We stopped our horses, leaned forward to rest our wrists on the saddle horn, and watched as they flitted and fluttered about.

The butterflies were attracted to our riding trail because the water they needed was there, as were mountains to protect them from the wind. They were also able to have a lovely feast of milkweed, goldenrod, and Queen Anne's lace.

In his garden every man may be his own artist without apology or explanation.
Here is one spot where each may experience "the romance of possibility."

LOUIS WILDER

With highways sprawling and land developments spreading, there are fewer and fewer places where butterflies can find the food and shelter they need, and protected butterfly habitats are becoming all the more important. To meet the needs of butterflies in your own garden, try planting red bee balm, zinnias, and a butterfly bush, for butterflies are attracted to color first. Like hummingbirds, they also need a still water source, such as a birdbath and a few large stones placed in the sun for them to sit upon and dry their wings. Keep the butterfly garden between tall hedgerows or next to a building to offer protection from the wind. Butterflies travel so far in their little lifetimes, and they always are in need of a place to rest.

A Healing Garden

Flowers and herbs truly are medicine for the soul, but it seems they might be even more. I just returned home from a trip to China, the very heart of tea country. The ancient Chinese discovered that drinking boiled water prevented illness. According to legend, a leaf fell from a Chinese woman's tree into a pot of boiling water, but the woman drank it anyway and liked it. The plant *Camellia sinensis* was first cultivated in China, and the drinking of tea soon spread throughout the Orient and beyond. Today, one of the most popular varieties in China is ginger root tea. I saw it advertised on billboards and sold throughout street markets. I learned that a warm mug of this herbal tea is not only full of flavor but also contains many restorative qualities. Ginger has been used for centuries as a mild stimulant to promote good circulation and to aid in digestion.

EASY INSPIRATION WATER GARDENS

A small fountain tucked into the corner of a tiny garden, apartment, or yard with limited space is perfect for a serene spot of inspiration. They require very little maintenance, yet are so rewarding. The element of water is the focus, so a fountain does not have to be big in size to have a big impact.

Fill a large terra-cotta saucer with water and float duckweed on top. Duckweed multiplies rapidly, for all it needs is standing water.

Fill a galvanized tub with water and fragrant blooming water hyacinths.

Float water lettuce on the top of a large terra-cotta planter. Seal the drainage hole to keep the water in.

A birdbath with pansy blooms and a floating candle is serene and soothing. The good news is that a birdbath does not always have to be outside! A concrete birdbath can add instant charm to an indoor garden setting.

Line a wooden barrel with a black plastic flowerpot, and float miniature water lilies in the pot.

A ready-made, tabletop fountain makes for an enjoyable goldfish home.

Keep a bar of soap outside on a nice flat rock near the water spigot. It is wonderful to be able to wash your hands off when they are especially muddy without having to go inside.

In his garden every man may be his own
artist without apology or explanation.
Here is one spot where each may
experience "the romance of possibility."

LOUIS WILDER

An ancient Chinese tea is wonderful to drink here at home for a brief respite during a busy day. I like to add four slices of ginger root to a cup of boiling water. Then I let it steep to deepen the flavor and sweeten it with a little honey. A slice of lemon or fresh orange is good, too.

A Moonlit Garden

An evening stroll through the garden can be most rewarding and romantic with a planting of all-white flowers. Even on a muggy hot summer's day, a white garden remains cool and refreshing. I like to weave a strand of white twinkling Christmas tree lights through climbing vines to imitate fireflies. White flowers are quite noticeable in the daylight hours, but they become serenely luminous in the glow of moonlight.

I wove twinkling lights through the wisteria vines that cover the railing of our boat dock and, with a few candles lit, it is a most relaxing place to end the day. The lights on our dock are plugged into a timer that turns them on just after dark. If I am up the hill in the house, the lights beckon me to come down and watch the evening stars and enjoy a scene of serenity in my garden.

The lesson I have thoroughly learnt, and wish to pass on to others, is to know the enduring happiness that the love of a garden gives.

GERTRUDE JEKYLL

Joys come from simple
and natural things;
mists over meadows,
sunlight on leaves,
the path of the moon over water.

SIGURD F. OLSON

4

A Garden for All Seasons

The pleasures of each season in the garden are ever-changing as one season evolves into the next. In the spring, I find it is the anticipation of awakening that captures my imagination. The promise of a garden lies just beneath the sleeping soil, and as the soft spring rains come, the mystery and joy seem to unfold on a daily basis. I check my summer garden every day that I am home. Because I travel quite a bit, it is so fun to see the changes that have happened while I was away. Upon returning home from a trip, I set my suitcase down on the doorstep and head immediately to the garden to savor its scent and glory. As late summer days grow short and the scent of fall is in the air, I keep busy putting my garden to

Memory is the ability to grow roses in the winter.

ANONYMOUS

bed. When winter finally arrives and it is too cold outside for both my flowers and me, I hibernate indoors, planning what to plant next spring.

Garden Rooms

To feel at home outdoors, we need to decorate our gardens so that they feel more like home. As I flip through the pages of gardening magazines, I notice that the trend is to let the interior of a home flow to the outside with beautifully appointed gardening "rooms." With the advent of air conditioning and television, it seems that we have gravitated indoors, especially in the summers. Now, we are moving our interests back outside in appreciation of the outdoors. No matter what the season, the garden is an extension of the home. When the coldest of winter days abound, the essence of my garden is in my home.

A most enjoyable addition to our home has been the addition of outdoor "rooms." Depending on your available space and needs, you may wish to create a special place for sitting, reading, napping, dining al fresco, or entertaining. It is easy to extend the borders of your home by creating little intimate spaces.

*How do you like to
go up in a swing,
Up in the air so blue?
Oh, I do think it the
pleasantest thing
Ever a child can do!*

*Up in the air and
over the wall
Till I can see so wide,
Rivers and trees and
cattle and all
Over the countryside—*

*Till I look down on
the garden green,
Down on the roof
so brown—
Up in the air I go
flying again,
Up in the air and down!*

ROBERT LOUIS
STEVENSON

Spacious suburban backyards, cozy front porches, and sunny poolside patios can all become outdoor rooms with welcoming furnishings that create comfortable living spaces. It seems that the lines of decorating are getting quite blurred, for we are bringing outdoor furniture in and indoor furniture out. When I hung a porch swing on an overhead beam in our guest house, my husband thought I had gone over the edge, but plump with pillows and a quilt, it has turned out to be a favorite spot for watching television. Swings have such a calming influence, for they remind us of oak trees and childhood dreams.

Old iron gates, picket fences, and garden benches add garden style either indoors or out. A friendly green wooden park bench says "welcome" when dressed with chintz and cottage rose pillows. Bird cages, birdhouses, architectural details, and watering cans have all become indoor and outdoor decorating accessories that extend our homes and our living spaces out into the garden. Instead of our families being separated from nature, it seems that more and more we are embracing the natural world with open arms.

Like winds and sunsets, wild things were taken for granted until progress began to do away with them.

A. LEOPOLD

The condominium balcony can be every bit as functional as a grand gazebo. The secret to such a simple cityscape is that it must appeal to all of our senses. Decorating the outside garden with the same loving attention you give the inside rooms can expand your home and make it as inviting as it is useful. Even a modest apartment balcony can accommodate a place to sit, enjoy the view, or sip a cup of tea and become a welcome extension with the addition of a few garden "pleasures." Choose a French bistro table and chair for dining and reading the morning paper with coffee, or a chaise lounge for relaxing with a novel. Add the elements of fragrant candlelight and a few well-chosen plants. Bird feeders perched on the edge of the privacy fence or hanging from a rooftop will become delightful sources of entertainment. Bring water into your garden "room" with a small birdbath nestled in the corner and filled with water and floating candles, or invest in a tabletop fountain with its soothing sound. A single full Boston fern can give a lush appearance to a tiny space. You can easily create a sense of intimacy if you have room for a small terra-cotta chiminea, or outdoor fireplace. A grouping of candles extends the enjoyment of the garden into the evening hours to make the very most of a tiny space.

New Life for Old Treasures

The French call it *élan*—an offhand elegance that lends charm to a room or a day. Bringing in a touch of the past with new uses for castoffs and old treasures adds a bit of surprise and whimsy to my garden. With a gathering of treasures, *élan* can be the key to an inspired garden. Especially in the wintertime, study the bones of the garden,

UNDER THE CLOAK OF WINTER

I always must have something green in the house, especially in the winter. This year I started a sweet potato plant in January. I cut a sweet potato in half and rooted it in a goldfish bowl. The goldfish seemed to enjoy the roots dangling down, and the sprouts captured our attention as they grew under the cloak of winter. When spring arrives, I will have a sweet potato vine to plant in the outdoor kitchen window box. It will flourish in the summer, with a cascading display of showy bright green leaves that contrasts nicely with the annuals. To grow your own sweet potato plant, you will need:

1 small sweet potato
8 round wooden toothpicks
1 glass Mason jar

Cut the sweet potato in half, and secure toothpicks around the raw edge. Place the raw side of the potato in water in the Mason jar. (The toothpicks should hold it an inch or so down under the water.) Set it in a windowsill and watch for budding to occur. Keep the water level above the edge of the potato so it does not dry out. In the spring, plant it in the dirt, roots and all. I enjoy watching the vine grow in the winter, and it is ready for my window box in the spring.

and then invest in birdbaths, sundials, and other garden art as focal points. Not only are these garden accents maintenance free, but they also add design structure and personality to a winter's garden.

In an intimate conversation spot in my garden sit two bent willow chairs with their arms draped in quilts. Overhanging limbs from a gracious oak tree hold a vintage chandelier that once was in someone's dining room and now graces my outdoor living room.

An overhead chandelier sets the stage for an evening's gathering. Even by daylight, a candle-filled chandelier hanging from a low branch causes me to look up at it and wish for the pleasure of an evening's idyll. A candle chandelier on the porch hanging over a skirted dining table or an outdoor picnic table sets the stage for entertainment. When decorating for Christmas,

I tuck in branches of holly and a red velvet ribbon. In the spring a few sprigs of Spanish moss drizzle down, as if it were growing. My outdoor chandelier is a joy all year long!

A hunt for the perfect chandelier need not take very much time or money, for in remembering the past, a flea market find with good "bones" will do. It can be easily spray painted — white, flat black, or left to just "weather" in the outdoor setting. With wire pliers, strip and remove any leftover wiring. You can purchase extra hanging chain and a plant hook from a hardware store. Place candles to burn where lightbulbs once glowed, and hang your chandelier low enough to illuminate your romantic evening garden.

Garden treasures are so fun to discover, especially when they come from your own past. Awhile ago, I found a box of chipped dishes in one of my mother's old toss away boxes. Immediately I recognized the pattern on the dishes, for they had been used at every meal growing up. Mother had grown tired of the Homer-Laughlin pattern plates, but I was delighted to rediscover them and display them in my outdoor garden rooms. The platter hangs over my potting-shed sink, one saucer acts as a coaster on a twig table, another dinner plate is on the baker's rack standing on end behind a fern. Not only are these old-fashioned plates charming with their swirled rose-pattern edges, but they warm my heart in turning back the clock.

A secondhand galvanized washtub adds country charm to a garden. These can be picked up quite inexpensively, and they are very versatile. The aged ones with holes rusted in the bottom are my favorite, for they can hold wood next to the outdoor fire without collecting rainwater. A washtub makes for an instant country garden when filled with an abundance of petunias cascading over the rim. The planter's rusty holes allow for proper drainage if they are filled with dirt. For a party, fill a clean tub with holes in the bottom with ice and drinks. The holes allow the melted ice water to drain, and the ice lasts longer.

Fire in the Night

It seems that firelight makes any room—indoors or out—a bit cozier. A setting takes on a special glow when bathed in candlelight. No matter what the season, you can enjoy the outdoors late into the evening with the addition of flickering flames. They not only create an intimate atmosphere, but also help to define a path or seating area and ward off pesky mosquitoes. Romantic candlelight can be brought into your garden with outdoor chandeliers or flea market candlesticks. Garden torches, votive candles, outdoor fireplaces, and floating candles for the water garden all add warmth to the evening atmosphere.

There is just something about fire that

NATURAL FIRE STARTERS

A year's worth of leftover candles, especially ones where the wick is all used up, do not have to go to waste. They can become quite useful fire starters if you melt them and dip pinecones in the wax. With adult supervision, they are a fun project for children and an inexpensive yet thoughtful gift. As the days grow short, fire starters are great for the holidays. All you need is:

*a large basket of pinecones
a double boiler
a gathering of old candles
a few drops of cinnamon oil
tongs
wax paper*

Melt the wax pieces in the top of a double boiler that has been filled with water in the bottom. Add a few drops of the cinnamon fragrance oil to the wax. Using the tongs, dip one pinecone at a time into the wax and place on wax paper to cool. Pinecones may be dipped several times for a buildup of wax, if desired. Place finished pinecones in a basket by the fireplace, ready for an evening fire, or tie them with a red velvet ribbon for the giving.

A YEAR IN FLOWERS

January — Snowdrop
February — Primrose
March — Violet
April — Daisy
May — Hawthorne
June — Rose
July — Water Lily
August — Poppy
September — Morning Glory
October — Hops
November — Chrysanthemum
December — Holly

beckons us to draw near. An outdoor fireplace extends the season with its added warmth. The flame, the fragrance, and the crackle of a campfire call to our hearts and cause us to linger. Outdoor fireplaces are quite popular, especially the terra-cotta ones called chimeneas, for they can burn wood in the winter and candles in the summer. It is the flickering flame that is so appealing no matter what the season. If you live in an area that does not permit open outdoor campfires, the adobe chimenea with its enclosed fire area is especially nice and safe for windy evenings. When you enjoy outdoor living, having an outdoor fireplace is like bringing the living room outside to you. It creates a cozy conversation spot to warm up your evenings. In warm climates where fireplaces are rarely needed, the romance of a flickering flame causes us to linger on crisp fall evenings or starry winter nights.

Our family's favorite gathering spot in the fall is down by the lake where we have created an open campfire pit. We love to roast marshmallows and hot dogs by the fire. My husband sometimes throws on a seasoned metal grate to cook steaks. A tripod holding a cast iron Dutch oven cooks a pot of October chili. And it seems that no matter the age of our guests—teenagers or seniors—the campfire has a universal appeal as an enjoyable spot to gather together and spend the evening.

I find it so mesmerizing to watch campfire flames dance in the darkness and listen to the sound of the crack-ling wood. Some woods I would never burn in my inside fireplace, but outdoors it is just fine—preferred, even—to burn pine, sweet gum, fir, and cedar. The sound of the fire pop-pop-popping and the smell of the wood smoke make for a relaxing, memorable setting in which to lie back on a quilt and gaze at the stars in the sky.

Ye shall say unto this mountain,
Remove hence to yonder place;
and it shall remove;
and nothing shall be
impossible unto you.

THE BOOK OF MATTHEW *(KJV)*

5

Wonders Never Cease

I t was the week of spring break for Samuel and Mason, and our destination was a cross-country tour to the Grand Canyon. At two-thirty in the morning my husband and I, along with both our boys, eagerly awaited the start of our planned adventure. We arrived at the Amtrak train station with bags packed and listened for the train's arrival in the early morning quiet.

The train finally arrived over an hour late, and it slowed into the station just long enough for us to hop on board with luggage in hand. We were assigned to our sleeper cars, and despite our excitement it did not take long for the train's motion to lull us to sleep.

The train window was at my head as I lay snuggled warm and cozy in the sleeping berth. Opening my eyes

*And this our life,
exempt from public haunt
Finds tongues in trees,
books in running brooks,
Sermons in stones and
good in everything.*

WILLIAM
SHAKESPEARE

from a peaceful slumber, I couldn't believe that although we were in the middle of a Kansas snowstorm, the train went right on through it as if it were only rain. As the day progressed, we took our meals in the dining car and enjoyed the passing scenery in the viewing car. We were treated to a front-row seat as we watched the tiny towns that dotted the landscape speed by. For miles and miles, we saw only flatlands and telephone poles. The lay of the land progressed as our train sped farther west through foothills with snowcapped mountains off in the distance.

We arrived at our evening stop, Williams Junction, late in the night and seemingly out in the middle of nowhere, where a lone shuttle bus awaited to take us to our hotel. The next morning we rode the Grand Canyon express railway another sixty miles along with several guitar-toting, singing cowboys. Finally it pulled into our destination —the original 1910 log station on the south rim of the Grand Canyon.

I like to think of nature as an unlimited radio station, through which God speaks to us every hour, if we will only tune in.

GEORGE
WASHINGTON
CARVER

I had seen the Grand Canyon pictured in books, magazines, and even movies, but absolutely nothing could have prepared me for such an experience looking out over God's creation. I was amazed at this magnificent canyon reaching as far in the distance as the eye can see. Looking deep below into the canyon, it was only with binoculars that I could barely make out the Colorado River. The awesome sight rendered all of us speechless as we stood in reverence over our first-time view.

Our guide shared with us his knowledge of the region's plant and animal life. How anything could thrive in this barren landscape of rock and wind was truly astonishing to me. We were treated to a sighting of four endangered California condors, of which we were told there were less than one hundred in existence. Effortlessly they hovered overhead, caught in a warm air current with their great wings spread.

The trees grew out of cracks and crevices in the rocks, where it seemed as if absolutely nothing should be growing. Our guide

Every happening, great and small, is a parable whereby God speaks to us and the art of life is to get the message.

MALCOLM
MUGGERIDGE

A BIRDHOUSE TO SHARE

Just a handful of planted seeds will produce delightful homegrown gourd birdhouses. To be able to "grow" your own birdhouse is a joy, and the seeds of a bottleneck gourd planted on a fence row will produce a fall bounty that is enough to share with friends and neighbors.

Gourds can be harvested in late summer or early fall after the vines have withered. Leave the stems attached to the gourds, and place them in a warm, sunny spot or in a dry attic for about three winter months. During this time the gourd will mold as it dries, and almost look as though it is rotting, but this is part of the natural curing process. If it rattles when you shake it, the gourd has dried enough to become a birdhouse.

I like to scrub my gourds with hot, soapy water and then scrape them to remove the dull, mottled coating that has developed. Rubbing them with a little steel wool gives a smooth, flawless finish, and then they are ready to dry.

The size I make the hole depends on the type of bird I am trying to attract. In general, I drill a two-inch hole at a center point of the gourd for the entrance and a couple of tiny pinholes in the bottom for drainage and ventilation. With a little prodding, the seeds of the gourd can be gently shaken out of the larger hole to be dried and saved in an envelope for sharing and planting again.

You can spray the gourd with a quick coat of clear polyurethane or dip it in a wood preservative and then allow it to dry. If I want to paint my gourd, I've found that an enamel white house paint works best. Either way, gourds need to be properly preserved so that they can last from one season to the next. Some of mine have lasted for several years.

With wire, hang the prepared gourd ten to twelve feet high with the hole facing out in the open. I have found that several gourds hung together attract purple martins the best. As summer ends, the gourd birdhouses can be shaken clean and put away for the winter. I store mine in the barn, clean and ready for spring.

told us that some of the trees were documented to be over five hundred years old, so not only did they grow—they thrived.

I could not imagine how trees could grow from seemingly solid rock. I was truly fascinated by the stones that were under our feet. Later that evening and still in awe, we sat on our chosen boulders to watch the sun go down. The sermon before our eyes: "Isn't it amazing what you can accomplish when you don't know what you can't do?" The trees grew out of stone because no one told them it was impossible. The Grand Canyon, God's Great Garden, served as our sermon in stone to show us that we too could do things we did not know were possible.

A Vacation Garden

I love to create a special corner of the garden with plants and treasures—even just a rock or a shell—that bring back memories from trips and vacations. I always try to bring home a cutting, seed, or memento from each one of our travels. From our vacation to the Grand Canyon, we brought back a stone large enough to write the date and the words "Grand Canyon." With a permanent felt tip marker, the writing will last for years even in the sun and rain. I placed the stone near the fishpond, along with our other vacation stones. Grouped together, they bring back memories of special times and special places that won't be forgotten when fall leaves cover the ground.

Oh! The things which happened in that garden! If you have never had a garden, you cannot understand, and if you have had a garden, you will know that it would take a whole book to describe all the things that came to pass there.

FRANCES HODGSON
BURNETT

My gardening friend Demi spent a recent vacation helping her friend Carolyn settle into a new home. Carolyn had moved several hours away, and she and Demi spent the week transplanting and planting together. It made the new home feel as though she had brought some touches of the

62

past with her to a new place. After Demi returned home, Carolyn still called her with frequent gardening reports— "The lilies are coming up" —and the two friends exchange Christmas gifts of wind chimes, birdhouses, and gardening books. Demi had a memorable vacation, and Carolyn has a very warm spot in her heart when she looks out upon her garden of flowers and friendship.

Gates Full of Surprise

Garden gates have always captured my attention, for most announce "welcome." My grandmother's country gate always closed on its own because of the simple chain that had a rock weight dangling on the end. Besides the garden gate, I also fondly remember the bleeding heart plants that greeted all those who entered the gate. This flower captivated my imagination, and now—even as an adult—it still fascinates me with its heart-shaped blossoms that dangle ever so gracefully from the stems.

> *Yes, the sowing of a seed seems a very simple matter, but I always feel as if it were a sacred thing among the mysteries of God.*
>
> CELIA THAXTER

My grandmother once shared with me the wonder and surprise inside the bleeding heart bloom. Pulling a single plucked blossom gently apart, she said, "This is what you'll get for Christmas. Two pretty pink rabbits, a pair of ballerina slippers, two fishing hooks for Daddy, and a baseball bat." With my imagination, it was easy to see the surprise each blossom held.

Sometimes the bleeding heart is called a lady's locket, for it suggests such with its deep rosy-red and pink candy heart blossoms. There is no mystery to the fanciful flowering plant, for it simply got its name from the outer petals that form a tiny heart, while inside a tiny inner petal "bleeds" its tip.

Look at the birds. They don't plant or harvest. They don't save food in houses or barns. But God takes care of them, and you are worth much more than the birds.

THE BOOK OF LUKE

The bleeding heart is original to the Orient, and a British botanist, Robert Fortune, brought home from his excursion a single plant. The bleeding heart suggests an old-fashioned garden that gladdens a cottage, and history proves how gardeners were captivated with the charming plant. It adapted well to England's climate and soon adorned many Victorian gardens. I planted one in my garden just to remind me of the one that always greeted visitors in the spring at my grandmother's enchanting gate.

I love to discover garden secrets and surprises, and my dad is a wonderful source for introducing me to them. Walking toward

our horse barn and by the pasture gate one fall day, the two of us discovered yet another surprise underneath the persimmon tree laden with fruit. Taking care to eat only the persimmons that were fully ripe, I bent over and searched for more that had fallen to the ground since the frost. I was in a hurry, until my dad said, "Look." Spitting out the seed, Daddy showed me how to split it carefully in half. Persimmon seeds look like an almond in size and color, but when a seed is split in two, a little imagination reveals a fork, a knife, or a spoon. Truly, wonders never cease, for it is when I am in the kitchen making persimmon cookies that I treasure the gift of time spent with my dad at the pasture gate.

A GARDEN BED AND BREAKFAST

Besides offering birds a home in the garden, you can also offer them food. A pinecone bird feeder is fun to make on a winter's day. Children especially love to make these. Just watching the birds fuss over this treat is wonderful wintertime enter-tainment! You will need:

3-6 large, dry, open pinecones
peanut butter
assorted birdseed
wire for hanging

With a spatula, spread and pack the peanut butter into the pinecone. Pour the birdseed into a large, round mixing bowl. Roll the peanut butter pinecone in the birdseed until it is coated with seed, then place it on wax paper and proceed with the next one. Loop a wire around the top of each pinecone and let it drop about twelve inches. Hang the other end of the wire on a tree limb and watch the fun begin. Cardinals and chickadees seem to favor sunflower seeds. Tiny black-capped chickadees and finches love thistle seed. Plan your seeds around the type of bird you are trying to attract.

Whoever sows sparingly
will also reap
sparingly, and whosoever
sows generously
will also reap generously.

THE BOOK OF
2 CORINTHIANS

6

A Bouquet of Gatherings

On the first day of May, my mother and I used to gather spring flowers from her garden. Sometimes they were just a fistful of delicate wildflowers from a spot in our yard. We would bring them into the house and arrange them simply in a tin can lined with a white lacy paper doily. We would then tie on a pretty satin ribbon bow for a handle. My treat was running to our elderly neighbor's door, placing the flowers over the doorknob, ringing the doorbell, and then hiding behind her bushes. Mrs. Barnes would always act as if she did not know I was there, even though she heard my giggles. Today, I cherish the May Day lesson of anonymous giving that Mother took time to teach me.

Where innocent bright-eyed daisies are, With blades of grass between, Each daisy stands up like a star Out of a sky of green.

CHRISTINA ROSSETTI

Even in our office and business surroundings, we can still revive the childhood pleasures of May Day and perhaps anonymously set a bud vase filled with wildflowers on a coworker's desk. A bouquet of blossoms from your garden may be just the thing to brighten an elderly neighbor's day. I don't know of anyone who does not like flowers, for they can bring a smile like nothing else. When my boys were little, we used to surprise their teachers now and then with a few flowers from our garden for their desks. It's so fun to revive an old tradition with a childlike handful of flowers for someone else.

Entertaining in the Garden

Easter, May Day, Mother's Day, birthdays, graduations —spring is just full of reasons to entertain in the garden. With flowers in bloom and plantings abundant, much of the decorating for a party is already done. The one thing that we do have to consider, though, is the weather. From experience, I have learned that Plan B is always an option!

On the morning of our annual Easter egg hunt this year, the skies looked like rain. We held fast to our plan of hiding the eggs outside, but planned to serve refreshments under the awning. The rain did come that day, and so did the children. But weather did not dampen our spirits or harm the plastic, candy-filled eggs. And the ducks and geese reveled in it! The decorations were spring flowers, made all the prettier by the rain. We huddled under cover to eat cookies and drink lemonade and decided that, all in all, the egg hunt was probably even more memorable for the children because of the spring rain.

> *In the door yard fronting an old farm-house near the white-washed palings, Stands the lilac-bush tall frowning with heart-shaped leaves of rich green, With many a pointed blossom, rising, delicate. with the perfume strong I love, With every leaf a miracle...*
>
> WALT WHITMAN

Most of our family members celebrate their birthdays in the spring. Gifts for the gardener are easy, so I always know what to get my father, sister, and sons—anything related to gardening, and they are pleased. My sister always loves to receive one of my antique jaunt "finds"—this year it was a vintage tablecloth printed with bright red cherries for her new covered patio.

In decorating for outdoor living, consider the rustic appeal of twig tables and chairs to blend with whatever your style. Colorful fabric pillows abundant with flowers can instantly give your garden "bloom." Antique shops and summer craft fairs are always wonderful decorating sources. A vintage cotton tablecloth and a watering can centerpiece filled with freshly picked flowers add a dash of festivity for unexpected guests.

All winter long I look forward to that first opportunity to dine outdoors. Depending on the weather where you live, spending time outdoors is a real treat after staying in all winter. In certain fortunate areas of the country, you can entertain outdoors all year long.

For the ease of entertaining, I like dishes that can be prepared ahead of time. That way, when guests begin to arrive, I can greet them at the door, offer a glass of lemonade, and spend time showing them the garden.

And those who are peacemakers will plant seeds of peace and reap a harvest of goodness.

THE BOOK OF JAMES

Through all my urban travels, I have come to appreciate the garden and its daily lessons more and more. From the hills of Hong Kong, where every inch of ground is a treasure and a possible garden spot, to the abundant window box and rooftop gardens of New York City, the miracle of planting a seed is just the same everywhere as it is in my own backyard. My work in my garden will never be done, but that is part of the joy. My fascination with the planting of every seed and the unfolding of every leaf is nothing short of a miracle. The friendships forged and the family memories created in the garden are the sweetest bouquets ever. May the flowering of friendships and memories within your garden bring you peace love, joy, and all that is good.

> *For the winter is past, the rain is over and gone. The flowers are springing up and the time of the singing of birds has come. Yes, spring is here.*
>
> THE SONG OF SOLOMON

Earth changes, but thy soul and God stand sure.

ROBERT BROWNING

Evening Dinner in the Garden

MENU

Flower Pot Salad with Vinaigrette Dressing
Fried Green Tomatoes
Fresh Corn Pudding
Green Bean Roll-ups
Baked Chicken Parmesan
Angel Biscuits with Fresh Strawberry Preserves
Chocolate-Dipped Shortbread Cookies with Freshly Sliced Peaches
Luscious Lemonade or Iced Tea

FLOWERPOT SALAD

New six-inch terra-cotta flowerpots make perfect salad bowls. Sitting on a china salad plate along with a saucer and a white paper doily, they set a perfect gardening theme.

4 new, six-inch terra-cotta flower pots with saucers, washed (I like to run mine through the dishwasher before using)
1 bunch red leaf lettuce, torn into bite-size pieces
1 bunch green leaf lettuce, torn into bite-size pieces
1 large cucumber, peeled and thinly sliced
1 cup grape tomatoes
1/4 cup pine nuts
1 small can sliced black olives
6 large basil leaves, chopped
6 green onions, cleaned and finely sliced
2 cups shredded mozzarella cheese

Combine all ingredients except for the cheese in large bowl and toss together. Refrigerate until ready to use. (This can be made a few hours ahead of time.) Just before serving, pour vinaigrette dressing over the top and toss again. Place salad servings in clean terra-cotta flowerpots. Sprinkle cheese on top. A nasturtium, pansy, or other edible flower makes a delightful garnish.

FLOWERPOT VINAIGRETTE DRESSING

Mix together 1 small bottle Zesty Italian salad dressing with 1/4 cup fresh, slightly mashed raspberries.

72

FRIED GREEN TOMATOES

In the spring it is hard to wait for the tomatoes to get ripe. Just like in the movie, fried green tomatoes are an act of love.

4 medium-size firm green tomatoes
2 eggs, beaten
1 cup seasoned Italian bread crumbs
2 tablespoons grated Parmesan cheese
1/4 teaspoon salt
1/4 teaspoon black pepper
2 1/2 cups solid vegetable shortening
wedges of fresh lemon

Wash, pat dry, and slice green tomatoes into half-inch thick slices. Make a dry mix of Italian bread crumbs, cheese, and salt. Dip the tomato slices into the beaten egg, and then dredge them in the dry bread crumb mixture. In a large heavy skillet, add enough short-ening to a depth of 1/2 inch and heat until it [shortening] is shimmering. Add half of the tomato slices. Lower the heat a little and cook covered until the bottoms of the tomatoes are browned (about 4 minutes). Turn the tomatoes over, then cover and cook for another 2 minutes. Drain on paper towels. Squeeze fresh lemon juice and a pinch of sugar on each tomato just before serving.

FRESH CORN PUDDING

6 ears of fresh corn, shucked and cut off the cob
1 small onion
salt and pepper to taste
2 tablespoons butter
1 cup cream
dash of nutmeg
1/4 cup basil, coarsely chopped
2 tablespoons butter, melted
3 egg yolks, beaten
3 egg whites, stiffly beaten

Shuck the ears of corn and remove the corn from the cob with a sharp paring knife. Scrape each cob to get all of the milk. (This will give you about 3 cups of corn). Sauté the corn, onion, and salt and pepper in butter for 5-8 minutes. Generously butter a one-quart baking dish. Mix the corn and onions with the other ingredients in the order given, folding in the egg whites last, and pour the mixture into a baking dish. Bake in a 300-degree oven for 35-40 minutes. Raise the heat to 375 degrees and brown on top for 10-15 minutes. This may be served hot or cold.

GREEN BEAN ROLL-UPS

2 pounds fresh, stringless pole
    beans, tips trimmed
1 tablespoon sugar
dash of garlic salt
1 pound sliced bacon
round wooden toothpicks
Cavenders seasoning
1-quart glass baking dish, greased

Wash beans well, then add them to boiling water along with sugar and garlic salt. Cook over medium heat for 30 minutes. Drain cooked green beans and let cool to touch. Cut bacon slices in half, to about 4-inch strips. Place 12-14 green beans in the palm of your hand. Wrap a bacon strip halfway around the bundle and secure it shut with a wooden toothpick. Place the bundle toothpick side down in the baking dish. Continue until all of the green beans and bacon have been used. Sprinkle roll-ups generously with Cavenders seasoning salt. Bake in a 300-degree oven for 20-30 minutes, or until bacon is cooked.

ICED TEA

When serving iced tea, rub a lemon wedge around the rim of the glass, then dip the rim in finely granulated sugar. Garnish with a sprig of mint.

FRESH STRAWBERRY PRESERVES

Leftovers of this make a quick, wonderful dessert spooned over vanilla ice cream.

4 quarts fresh-picked ripe
    strawberries
9 1/2 cups granulated sugar
1 large lemon

Cap strawberries, slice in half, and combine with sugar in a large mixing bowl. Cover and let stand overnight, then pour into a non-aluminum saucepan. Add the juice of one lemon and slowly heat to a boil while stirring constantly with a wooden spoon. Let the mixture simmer for five minutes. Put the strawberry mixture back in the mixing bowl, cover, and refrigerate for 24 hours. Return the mixture to the saucepan and bring it to a rapid boil until the syrup has thickened. (This takes about 30 minutes.) Cool and refrigerate until ready to use. Preserves may be frozen in airtight containers, or they will keep for several weeks in the refrigerator.

LUSCIOUS LEMONADE

Lemonade is the official drink of the garden. I have learned that it simplifies things to use lemonade drink mixes. I mix up the lemonade ahead of time so it is ready to be poured when the guests arrive. For a crowd, it is convenient to mix up a concentrated batch and let the ice melt to dilute it. The panache is in the presentation, for shiny glasses with a circle of sliced lemon floating on them are so inviting. I also like to float strawberries or raspberries in the lemonade, which looks so attractive served from an antique crystal pitcher. Clean, unsprayed pansies or sprigs of lavender float quite nicely on top, too.

BAKED CHICKEN PARMESAN

4-6 chicken breasts, split
1/2 cup flour
1/2 cup grated Parmesan cheese
1/2 teaspoon salt
1/2 teaspoon pepper
1/4 teaspoon garlic powder
2 teaspoons paprika
1/2 cup melted butter
1 egg
3 tablespoons milk

In a large mixing bowl, blend together flour, cheese, paprika, salt, pepper, and garlic powder. In a separate bowl, mix egg and milk together. Dip each chicken breast into the egg and milk mixture, then dredge it in the flour mix. Place coated chicken breasts in a shallow baking pan and drizzle the butter over each piece. Bake at 350 degrees for 1 1/4 hours, or until chicken is done.

CHOCOLATE-DIPPED SHORTBREAD COOKIES

3 cups all-purpose flour, sifted
1/2 teaspoon soda
1/2 teaspoon baking powder
1 cup butter-flavor shortening
2 eggs
1 cup sugar

In a large mixing bowl, combine flour, soda, and baking powder, then cut in the shortening. In a separate bowl, beat eggs, then add sugar. Stir well. Pour the egg mixture into the dry mixture and stir until dough forms.

Generously flour a cutting board and roll out dough to 1/4-inch thickness. Cut out heart shapes and transfer with a spatula to an air-bake cookie sheet. Bake at 375 degrees for 6-8 minutes. Remove from the oven and place cookies on a cooling rack.

To make the chocolate dip, melt 1 package of Hershey's milk chocolate baking bits in the top of a double boiler. When cookies are cool, dip just half of the cookie into the melted chocolate, then put back on the cooling rack. Serve cookies with freshly sliced peaches that have been sprinkled with sugar and Fruit Fresh to keep them from turning dark. Add a sprig of mint from your garden for garnish.

ANGEL BISCUITS

This recipe is one of my family's classics. It is so nice because it can be made ahead a day or two and kept in the refrigerator until ready to use. I always considered them a treat for either my family or my guests.

4 cups all-purpose flour
2 cups buttermilk
1 tablespoon sugar
2 teaspoons salt
1 teaspoon soda
3 level teaspoons baking powder
1 cup shortening
1 package dry yeast

Stir and dissolve the dry yeast in a teacup with a little warm water. In an electric mixer, mix half of the flour with all of the remaining ingredients. The gently mix in the last 2 cups of flour. Place the dough on a floured board and knead, adding flour as needed. Give the dough one hour to rise, then punch it down. At this point you can refrigerate the dough for later use or cut it into biscuit shapes and bake at 450 degrees for 10-12 minutes.

A Rose Garden Tea

MENU

Lemonade with Rose Petal Ice Cubes
Rose Hip Tea
Teatime Turkey Sandwiches
Brioche Rolls with Egg Salad
Garden Gates
Lady Fingers Sandwiches
Ever-Easy Walnut Brownies
Crescent Moons
Lemon Iced Candy

For an easy centerpiece, gather a few pansies, herbs, roses, or other dainty flower, using a teapot as a vase. I have several teapots with broken lids, and I have saved them just for this purpose. Certain herbs just lend themselves to tea—lemon balm, bee balm, pineapple mint, apple mint, chamomile, and lavender. The weather at a springtime rose garden tea might just be warm enough for you to serve iced drinks. Ice cubes with a rose petal frozen inside each cube look pretty floating in a glass of minty tea, a bowl of punch, or even a tumbler of lemonade.

ROSE PETAL ICE CUBES

Fill ice cube trays one-half full with water and freeze. Place a clean, pesticide-free rose petal on top of each cube. Fill the tray with just enough water to cover each petal, then freeze again to hold in place. Finally, fill the tray completely full of water and freeze. The ice cubes will be clearer if you use water that has been boiled rather than cooled —or leave some water sitting out overnight. This "flattens" the water and removes the air bubbles.

BRIOCHE ROLLS WITH EGG SALAD

4 hard-cooked eggs, finely chopped
1/4 cup mayonnaise
2 tablespoons spicy brown mustard
1 tablespoon chives, finely chopped
dash of garlic salt
dash of fresh ground pepper

Combine all ingredients in a large mixing bowl until blended. Split brioche rolls in half and spread both halves with mayonnaise. Fill with egg salad filling. Place on cookie sheet and cover tightly with plastic wrap until ready to serve.

ROSE HIP TEA

Did you know that even roses bear fruit? Their fruit is called "rose hips." Rose hips vary in size, depending on the type of rosebush. Birds such as robins, bobwhites, mockingbirds, and even pheasant feast on the rosy-colored hips. They are a wonderful addition to flower arrangements in the fall and winter. You can also enjoy a rose hip tea, for the hips are high in vitamin C. To make a cup of rose hip tea, pick the ripest berry-like hips off the autumn rosebushes. Wash them in mild, soapy water and rinse very well. Place them on paper towels to dry in a dark, warm space for about three weeks, then chop them finely in a food processor. (If they are still not completely dry, spread them out on a paper towel to dry them some more.) Store rose hips in a jar with a tight-fitting lid. To make the tea, steep 1 teaspoon of hips in a cup of boiling water. Boil for five minutes and pour through a tea strainer into a cup. Sweeten with sugar, if desired. Please take care not to use rose hips that have been sprayed or dusted with any kind of chemical.

LADY FINGERS SANDWICHES

1 loaf of sourdough sandwich
    bread, sliced
cream cheese at room temperature
2 medium cucumbers, peeled,
    seeded, and grated
1 small onion, grated
pepper
fresh dill, chopped

Spread cream cheese on both sides of bread, then sprinkle with dill. Place grated cucumbers and onions on top of the cream cheese, then put the tops on the sandwiches and trim off all four sides of the crust. Cut each sandwich into three or four ladyfinger sandwiches. Again, these may be prepared early and covered tightly, then refrigerated.

GARDEN GATES

1 loaf of cocktail rye bread
Vermont cheddar cheese, sliced
1 purple onion, thinly sliced
prepared gourmet chutney
    (I recommend Major Grey's
    mango chutney)

Layer the cheese on the cocktail bread with a paper-thin slice of purple onion. Add a teaspoon of fruit chutney, then top with another piece of bread. These may be prepared early and tightly covered, then refrigerated.

TEATIME TURKEY SANDWICHES

Tiny little bite-sized sandwiches are traditional for tea. Depending on the number of guests I have invited, I allow for at least six dainty sandwiches per guest. I like to keep the sandwiches simple, but simple is made wonderful by using the best and freshest of ingredients. Green scallion blades have a wonderfully gentle flavor and add color to these sandwiches. For either a garden party luncheon or bridal shower, these are some of my favorites. They can easily be prepared ahead of time.

1 loaf fresh raisin bread, thinly sliced
2 8-ounce packages of cream cheese at room temperature
1/2 cup scallions (both greens and white tips), finely chopped
fresh basil leaves
1/4 cup pecans, coarsely chopped
turkey breast, thinly sliced

Fold chopped scallions evenly into the cream cheese. Spread the cream cheese mixture onto both sides of the raisin bread, then lightly sprinkle each piece of bread with approximately 1 teaspoon of pecans. Layer four basil leaves over the cream cheese and pecans. Next, layer a thin piece of sliced turkey.

Place one of the sandwiches on top of the other with the cream cheese inside. Trim crusts and slice into triangles with a sharp knife. Set the sandwiches on a cookie sheet and place a damp paper towel over them. Cover with plastic wrap and refrigerate until ready to serve.

LEMON ICED CANDY

2 10-ounce packages of hard lemon drop candies
8 ounces vanilla candy coating

Preheat oven to 300 degrees. Place lemon drops in a Ziploc bag and crush with a rolling pin. Spread the crushed candy on a lightly greased jellyroll pan. Bake for 12 minutes or until candy is nicely melted. Tilt the pan to cover all of the edges and thin out the candy, then let it cool in the pan. Melt the vanilla candy coating in a nonstick saucepan, stirring constantly. Spread the vanilla coating evenly over the lemon candy layer. Chill in the refrigerator for 15-20 minutes, then break into assorted bite-size pieces.

CRESCENT MOONS

1/2 cup butter
1/2 cup powdered sugar
1/2 teaspoon vanilla
1/4 teaspoon almond extract
1 cup pecans, chopped
1 cup all-purpose flour

Cream butter with sugar, vanilla, and almond extract until light and fluffy. Add half of the nuts and fold in evenly. Add flour and remaining nuts. Blend well. Shape a one-inch ball of dough into crescents. Place on an ungreased cookie sheet and bake at 325 degrees for 20 minutes. Cool on a wire rack. Roll in powdered sugar to coat well.

EVER-EASY WALNUT BROWNIES

Chocolate, I have decided, must be a vegetable since it comes from a bean. There can never be enough chocolate, for it is appropriate for any season or any reason. This family recipe is one to always keep close at hand, even if it is just you alone with a cup of tea and a brownie. What could be better?

1/2 cup butter
4 ounces unsweetened chocolate, grated
4 large eggs
1/4 teaspoon salt
2 cups granulated sugar
1 teaspoon vanilla extract
1 cup all-purpose flour
1 cup walnuts, chopped

Melt together butter and chocolate in a small, heavy saucepan. Let the butter and chocolate mixture cool. With an electric mixer, beat together eggs and salt until foamy (3-4 minutes). Pour the chocolate and butter mixture into the egg and salt mixture, then mix on medium speed. Add the sugar and vanilla until well mixed. With a wooden spoon, fold in the flour and walnuts. Pour the mixture into a buttered, 13 x 9 inch cake pan and bake at 350 degrees for about 30 minutes, or until a wooden toothpick inserted comes out with cooked crumbs attached to it.

For a picnic, I cut these into larger squares, but for a garden tea party, two-inch, bite-size squares are best. I like to line a plate with real leaves (washed) and top it with a lacy doily. Then I place the brownies on the doily and dust lightly with powdered sugar. Serve on a plate garnished with a few ripe strawberries.